Can I tell you about Down Syndrome?

Can I tell you about...?

The 'Can I tell you about...?' series offers simple introductions to a range of limiting conditions and other issues that affect our lives. Friendly characters invite readers to learn about their experiences, the challenges they face, and how they would like to be helped and supported. These books serve as excellent starting points for family and classroom discussions.

Other subjects covered in the Can I tell you about...? series

ADHD

Adoption

Anxiety

Asperger Syndrome

Asthma

Autism

Cerebral Palsy

Dementia

Depression

Diabetes (Type 1)

Dyslexia

Dyspraxia

Eating Disorders

Eczema

Epilepsy

ME/Chronic Fatigue Syndrome

Nut Allergy

OCD

Parkinson's Disease

Pathological Demand Avoidance Syndrome

Peanut Allergy

Sensory Processing Difficulties

Selective Mutism

Stammering/Stuttering

Stroke

Tourette Syndrome

Can I tell you about Down Syndrome?

A guide for friends, family and professionals

ELIZABETH ELLIOTT
Illustrated by Manjit Thapp

Jessica Kingsley *Publishers*
London and Philadelphia

First published in 2016
by Jessica Kingsley Publishers
73 Collier Street
London N1 9BE, UK
and
400 Market Street, Suite 400
Philadelphia, PA 19106, USA

www.jkp.com

Library of Congress Cataloging in Publication Data
Elliott, Elizabeth J.
Can I tell you about Down syndrome? : a guide for friends,
family and professionals / Elizabeth Elliott.
pages cm -- (Can I tell you about...?)
Audience: Age 7+.
Audience: Grade 4 to 6.
Includes bibliographical references.
ISBN 978-1-84905-501-7 (alk. paper)
1. Down syndrome--Juvenile literature. I. Title.
RJ506.D68E45 2016
618.92'858842--dc23
2015017896

British Library Cataloguing in Publication Data
A CIP catalogue record for this book is available from the British Library

ISBN 978 1 84905 501 7
eISBN 978 0 85700 904 3

Printed and bound in Great Britain by Bell & Bain Ltd, Glasgow

This book is dedicated to my late father
Peter Elliott, who was an inspiration and fought
for over 20 years for quality medical research
to improve the quality of life of all people with
Down syndrome. He sought no recognition or
reward, only to help his son (and my brother),
David, and many others. He is greatly missed.

Acknowledgements

I would like to thank:

- David and our mum, Sylvia

- Brendan (my husband) and our family

- Hayley and Natty Goleniowska for their positivity in the DS community

- Editors Lucy Buckroyd and Emma Holak at Jessica Kingsley Publishers for their patience and the opportunity to create this book

- Manjit Thapp, for capturing David so well in this book.

Contents

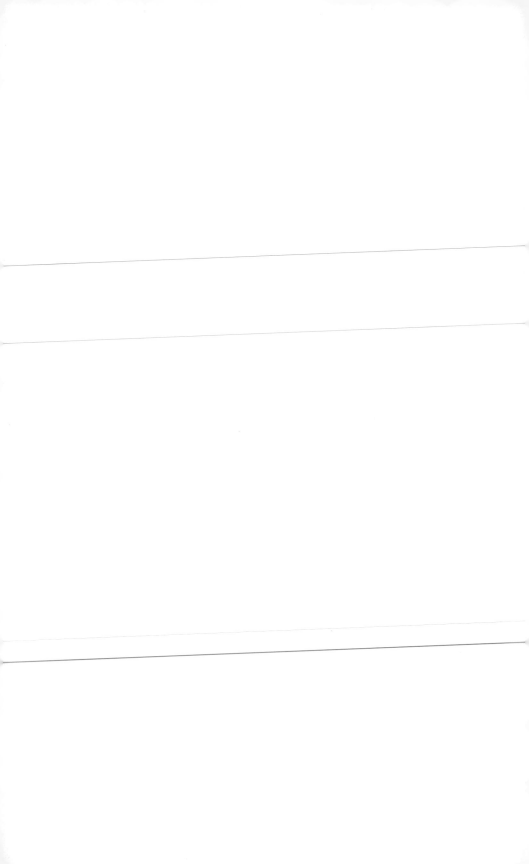

Introduction

This book was written to help older children and adults gain a better understanding of what life is like for someone with Down syndrome.

It will describe what Down syndrome is and, importantly, what it isn't.

We will learn about how people with Down syndrome are more often like us than they are different from us. We will also learn about the ways that they might need more support or consideration.

This book will also assist teachers and others in various settings (e.g. a workplace) to learn more about Down syndrome, stimulate conversation and develop a sensitive way to conceptualise and discuss Down syndrome.

We will learn about it from David, who is 12.

"Don't forget that I'm just David. Down syndrome is not the biggest part of me!"

"Hi, I'm David, nice to meet you! Welcome to my book. I'm going to tell you about something that has been a part of me since before I was born. It's called Down syndrome. Let's call it DS for short.

No, it doesn't mean I'm down or anything. A long time ago a man called John Langdon Down met lots of people like me and he realised we had a lot of similarities. So they called it Down's or Down syndrome after him. I wish his name was Awesome so I could say I have Awesome syndrome but it doesn't really matter because I am pretty cool anyway.

I will tell you about me and DS in my book and try to explain some stuff in case you meet someone with DS. I hope that by the end you'll know a lot more.

But the first, most important thing I want you to always remember: everyone with DS is a new and different person and it isn't the most important thing about them!

Got it? Great!"

"When I was made I got 47 chromosomes and you got 46!"

"My dad explained to me what DS is and why it makes me the same as and different from everybody else. Inside all the cells of your body you have the instructions to build and run your body. This is called DNA and it's twisted up into 46 chromosomes. They actually look like little people under a microscope!

Well, at the very beginning when I was created I got one extra chromosome, so I have 47! So in most ways my body runs the same as yours but in some ways it's different because it got extra instructions.

The first man to discover the extra chromosome was Dr Jerome Lejeune and he lived in Paris. I like him because he said 'Every patient is my brother' and he helped people with DS to be healthy and worked hard so people didn't treat us differently or try to get rid of or hide us away.

DS won't go away, it's just a part of who I am. And you can't catch it! It's like any other medical condition like asthma or diabetes. Most things about my day-to-day life are the same as yours so it's a special sort of medical condition that doesn't get worse or better, it's just there.

My dad always said that DS has meant I'm more determined and sometimes have to work harder than other people and that always made him very proud of who I am. "

"Well, that's a slightly tricky one, as everyone who has DS is affected by it differently. And don't forget what I said, we're all different people too.

There are some things that we do have in common though. Most of us with DS have some amount of learning difficulties. This means we take a little longer to learn some things, and for me it's reading and maths. But for other people with DS it might be something else they take longer to understand."

WHEN I WAS LITTLE...

"When I was a baby I went to groups called Portage and Early Intervention that helped things like my muscles and movement, which can take longer to get strong. My mum said I loved it. When I was little I needed longer to learn to walk than other babies.

Sometimes a baby with DS also has problems with their heart that might need an operation like my friend Natty. Once it's fixed normally they are fine and most times can run and play just like you."

"There are lots of ways to help
me communicate, but this is
one of my favourites!"

COMMUNICATION

"Many kids with DS have something called speech therapy to help them learn to talk a bit more clearly by learning mouth exercises. A lot of babies with DS learn some signs with their hands before they even learn to talk. It's pretty cool! I knew how to say 'thank you', 'please' and 'more' before I could ever talk just by using my hands.

Sometimes I do get frustrated when I can't explain stuff to my family or at school, it's like the words get stuck in my head. At times like that it helps to have patient people who ask questions or wait for me to describe what I'm trying to say.

Teachers might have special ways they help me to communicate like Makaton symbols or pictures too. My friend Tom with DS has an iPad at his school to help him communicate too."

NOW THAT I AM OLDER...

"I don't really do things like speech therapy or Portage anymore. Instead I keep active! Our local support group held a talk all about how physical activity is really important for people with DS. People with DS can have a something called low muscle tone and coordination issues. Exercise really helps us with this. Last year I was on the special needs basketball team and worked on improving my bike riding skills."

"Well, lots of stuff...and none of it has anything to do with DS! Does that surprise you? I like hanging out with my family and friends. We watch TV or movies and talk about them after. I like to imagine I'm a character in the movie.

My favourite show is Dr Who and I think David Tennant was the best Doctor. Some people with DS love watching the same movie loads, and I'm like that with my favourite Dr Who DVDs too. My uncle thought it was cool I even knew the words to most of it too!"

"I've got loads of hobbies. Sometimes
I can't decide what I want to do!"

"Personally I really like drawing and get ideas of what to draw everywhere. I've also done art with clay and stained glass. I've got my own style and people can always spot the things I've done.

During my last holidays I was learning to ski and I'm already better than my older sister. When I go I have two teachers who come with me to remind me of what I've learned in case I forget. Most of the time they're just there to be my 'back-up' and they don't have to do much.

I know some grown-ups with DS and they live in flats with other people around who are their 'back-ups' too. They pop in to lend a hand or just have a cup of tea and a chat. I can't wait to be older now.

I know a famous photographer who has DS and even actresses in big shows. So like 'normal' people, some people with DS have special talents and some are just famous in their own families!

I know all the stuff I like to do isn't because I have DS because other people I know with DS don't like the same stuff, so I think I'm just David."

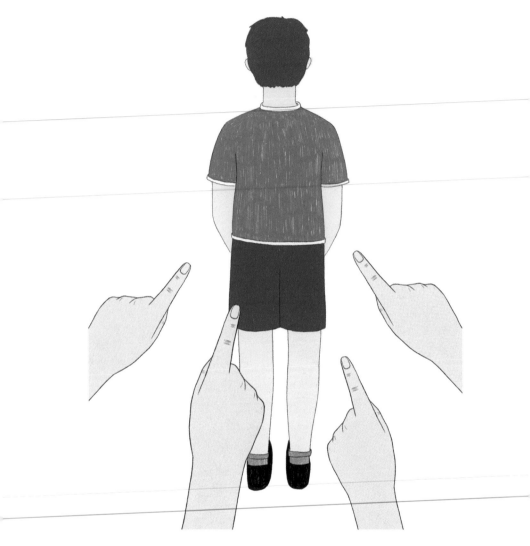

"No one wants to be picked
on and I'm the same!"

" Like you, I love being with my friends. I don't want to be friends with only people with DS. I like friendly, funny kids like me, I don't mind what conditions they might have, because we're all different, right?

There are some things I do want my friends or classmates to know about me though. Please don't make fun of me if I don't understand something because of my learning difficulties or DS. It makes me feel angry and sad and nobody likes to be picked on.

If you think someone is being unkind or bullying me or anybody else then my teacher said it's always important to tell someone in charge.

If there is a game starting, include me if I want to play. If I seem confused about the rules, please explain again, I might need a little longer to understand this game. Try not to get angry with me if I do misunderstand; that really helps.

The best times are when me and my friends do the things we love like playing football or watching Dr Who. These times don't seem to be about DS at all, just about having fun. "

"This is Amy, my classroom assistant.
We're just doing my homework."

"Some people with DS need to go to a school that is really good at helping people with different learning difficulties and some go to school with people with no learning difficulties (integration in a 'mainstream' school). I've done both and enjoyed both.

At the mainstream school a classroom assistant would sometimes sit with me and work on the lesson with me. Sometimes I would be doing the same work as the class but sometimes I worked on a different assignment on the same topic. It helped when my class didn't make me feel different because of this. Sometimes if people picked on me I would feel really sad. It helped if the teacher talked about us all being different and needing help at different times, then I didn't feel embarrassed.

When I went to a school with other people with learning difficulties (a 'special school') I had different challenges and experiences. The teachers were experts in helping people with various difficulties to learn. There is a timetable and classes just like a mainstream school but the classrooms and lessons were planned differently, to match our learning needs. In my smaller class group we'd cover the same topic but mostly our work was different, designed just for me at my stage. Just like my other school we all love break time best of all!

Like I mentioned communication can be tricky for me and some people with DS. When I was little the extra ways to communicate really helped, like Makaton pictures and hand signing. Now I'm a bit older I still sometimes need a little longer if I'm trying to explain or understand something complicated like setting up my TV to watch a DVD.

All this doesn't mean I need help doing everything though! I want to help others too, just like you. I help Mum and Dad all the time, especially in the garden when I can carry heavy stuff for my mum. Try not to rush in and do everything for me, I've learned lots when I've had to figure it out. "

"My teacher is telling the class
about DS. I really hope they
all still treat me the same."

"I know that people can tell there is something a bit different about me, and I get asked about it too. Sometimes I worry people won't like me because I have DS. Most of the time I don't even think about having DS, I just get on with doing the things I do.

When a teacher decides to talk about DS with my class I want to be there and reading a book like this will help them to express the important things about DS and the things which don't matter too much."

"I'm me, I'm David."

"I don't want people to see me and just see the 'Down syndrome kid' – I'm me, I'm David. So please think carefully about how you talk about it, maybe even waiting until the other children start to ask about it, because they might not have noticed anything.

Sometimes people tell my mum 'Ah, people with Down syndrome, they're so cuddly.' That is not true though! I get grumpy and lots of times I don't feel like being cuddly. I have all the same feelings as you do. So please don't tell my class everyone with DS is the same – they might get a shock!

The other thing that I want is to be treated the same as the rest of the class as much as possible. My timetable might be a bit different or I might have different homework than the other children. My mum also says if I'm rude I should get in trouble like anyone else. I feel like it's only fair that I don't have special rules. "

How teachers can help

- Reading this book is great first step. The more you can remove your set ideas about DS and me, the more I might surprise you. Please avoid the stereotypes such as that I am always happy or can't learn to do a specific thing.

GET TO KNOW HOW DS AFFECTS YOUR STUDENT'S NEEDS

- Reading my assessments and available information about my strengths and weakness can really help you to help me. Maybe your student with DS had a psychology assessment or one from a speech and language therapist. Sometimes this is all in my "Statement of Special Needs" so don't forget to read it.

- It will help you to know that there is an increased chance of other learning problems when someone has DS, for example dyslexia and autism. If you are concerned that someone with DS also has another condition ask for another opinion from your senior teacher. The sooner it's diagnosed the more my learning needs can be identified and met.

COMMUNICATION AIDS AND METHODS

- Your Special Education Coordinator (SENCO), educational psychologist or skilled teachers can help you use communication aids to improve my ability to express myself and for you to talk to me. Special courses and resources are available online to help you learn too!

INTEGRATION

- That's a fancy word for making sure I get a chance to mix with other children my age and I'm not kept separated with other kids with DS or disabilities. It's good for all children to meet and be able to play together.

KEEPING UP TO DATE

- It's great when my teacher knew tablets like iPads were great for helping children with DS learn reading and writing. She found this out because she said she likes "keeping up to date." She goes to special meetings and training to help me and others do our best at school.

How parents can help

IN THE BEGINNING

- When I was first born my parents were worried because they didn't know anything much about DS. Even worse, some parents are confused about it and think that people with DS won't walk or talk! My mum says she'd love a time machine to go back and tell herself "Don't worry, Sylvia!" when I was born because everything has been OK so far and I'm lovely. Sometimes there are tough days but she always says it's that way with all kids.

FEELINGS

- I asked mum if there were other things she'd like other parents to know about life with a kid with DS. She said that so much that she worried about never came true. That it was ok to cry and be upset, to not understand, and even be angry. But through all of this, the overwhelming feeling that comes to the surface is the joy and love they have for their child. And their child just becomes their child, not a syndrome, with their daddy's eyes or mummy's nose.

GET INVOLVED

- One of the best things my mum did was to get involved with playgroups for babies with DS and chat with other mums. She said it was great for her and me to make friends and ask questions. She's still friends with those people now, years later, and one lady is her best friend.

- Nowadays she's always talking about the Facebook group she's in with other mums of kids with DS. It's so embarrassing when she shares a photo of me! Last week she put up a pic of me skiing, but it is cool – it got 56 likes!

MY "SQUEAKY WHEEL"

- Sometimes Mum says she has to be my "squeaky wheel"! That means if she thinks I need extra help or services she'll talk to my teacher, doctor or anyone who can help. It's an important part of how my parents help to get what I need to be healthy or learn.

TALKING ABOUT DS OPENLY

- Lots of people still don't know or understand about DS and one time a mummy called her children away when we were playing and acted like I had a bad cold that they might catch. That made my mum sad. My parents and I want you to know that not all people are like that and most are kind or just curious. They might have questions and need you to explain and be patient with them.

BEST OF ALL

- The best thing about my mum and dad is when they have been proud of me doing stuff that maybe other parents don't even notice. They texted everyone they knew when I learned to ride a bike. I think it's nice and I always find it encourages me to keep learning new things.

How my siblings and family can help

- When I came along my big sisters and brothers were excited to meet me. At the start they didn't really understand that anything was different about me. They just thought I was cute but cried too much. Mum and Dad said sometimes they worried about how me having DS might be tricky for my siblings. Now we know most of the time it's just the same for them as it was before I was born. We get along some days and other days my sister bugs me so much!

- I'd tell other brothers and sisters out there to just get to know their sibling and be kids together. If your brother with DS learns signs you can learn a few too from your mum. Ask questions if you are wondering anything too – don't be shy.

- If someone with DS joins your family it will help to learn more about what someone with DS is really like and about the myths. A lot of people who knew my parents were nervous to ask or talk to my mum and dad about how everything was going when I was born. I'm glad my big family knew what to say and could teach others what was true and false about DS. If someone you know has a baby with DS, don't forget to call their mum or dad to say congratulations!

Recommended reading, organisations and websites

There is lots of great information out there for everyone who knows someone with DS.

PUBLICATIONS
Woodbine Books
Woodbine Books has a large selection of books for and about people with DS, in particular books for siblings and new parents.
Website: www.woodbinehouse.com

RESOURCES
Makaton
Makaton is a programme that uses signs and symbols to help people with special needs to communicate. They have printed and e-resources.
Website: www.makaton.org

See and Learn
Designed specifically for the learning needs of children with
DS, See and Learn teaching programs help parents and
educators with structured and individualized teaching. They
are designed for regular use at home and in the classroom,
and are available as physical kits or as apps.
Website: http://www.seeandlearn.org

Scope
Scope is a charity devoted to supporting disabled people and
their carers. Be sure to check out the community area of their
website for tips for carers and professionals.
Website: www.scope.org.uk

Mencap
Mencap is a charity offering a variety of services to people
with disabilities, their carers and professionals.
Website: www.mencap.org.uk

ORGANISATIONS
UK
Down's Syndrome Association
2 Langdon Park
Teddington
Greater London
TW11 9PS
Phone: +44 (0) 208 614 5100
Email: info@downs-syndrome.org.uk
Website: www.downs-syndrome.org.uk

This is the UK parental support organisation that can help
people with DS at all different stages of life. They have a
scheme to help match people with employers to get people
into work. They can also connect you with your local group.

Down Syndrome Research Foundation UK
42 Cleveland Gardens
London
NW2 1DY
Phone: +44 (0) 208 731 7880
Email: info@dsrf-uk.org
Website: www.dsrf-uk.org

The only UK charity dedicated to lobbying for and funding medical research to help people with DS. They also provide a free book for new parents called *Bright Beginnings*.

Down Syndrome Education International
6 Underley Business Centre
Kirkby Lonsdale
Cumbria
LA6 2DY
Phone: +44 (0) 300 330 0754
Email: info@dseinternational.org
Website: www.dseinternational.org

This charity is dedicated to raising levels of educational achievement among children with DS. They have publications, learning apps and plan to create online training.

USA

National Down Syndrome Society
666 Broadway
8th Floor
New York 10012
Phone: +1 800 221 4602
Email: info@ndss.org
Website: www.ndss.org

National Down Syndrome Congress
30 Mansell Court
Suite 108
Roswell
Georgia 30076
Phone: +1 800 232 6372
Email: info@ndsccenter.org
Website: www.ndsccenter.org

Australia

Down Syndrome Australia
219 Napier Street
Fitzroy
VIC 3065
Phone: 1300 881 935
Email: info@downsyndrome.org.au
Website: www.downsyndrome.org.au

International

Down Syndrome Pregnancy
Email: stephanie.meredith@uky.edu
Website: http://downsyndromepregnancy.org

Down Syndrome Pregnancy is a resource for Prenatal and Postnatal information on DS. They produce education and support for those preparing for the birth of a baby with Down syndrome and their loved ones. They produce Brighter Tomorrows, an online resource for new and expectant parents, and Lettercase, a programme for expectant parents first learning about prenatal screening/testing and a Down syndrome/Trisomy 21 diagnosis. An excellent resource.

Down Syndrome International
Langdon Down Centre
2A Langdon Park
Teddington
Middlesex
TW11 9PS
Phone: +44 (0)1392 357554
Email: contact@ds-int.org
Website: www.ds-int.org